Killing Orpheus

Killing Orpheus

* * *

Forester McClatchey

Carnegie Mellon University Press
Pittsburgh 2026

Acknowledgments

Grateful acknowledgments to the editors of the following journals where these poems first appeared, possibly in slightly different versions:

32 Poems: "Alpine Meadow"
The Baltimore Review: "Ophelia"
Bayou Magazine: "Reading Catullus in Bed"
Birmingham Poetry Review: "Stanzas for Dwoskin"
Booth: "Gall"
Crab Creek Review: "Penelope, Growing Old"
swamp pink (formerly *CrazyHorse*): "On the Nature of Yes"
Denver Quarterly: "Minnows"
The Ekphrastic Review: "The Albert Memorial"
Gulf Coast: "Root Words," "Ambivalence of Birds"
Gulf Stream: "Eating in a State of Flowers" (winner of Gulf Stream 2019 Summer Prize)
The Hopkins Review: "In a Green Shade"
Literary Matters: "Humdrumming," "Wild Azaleas," "Wringing Lilies from the Acorn"
minnesota review: "Coffee Grounds"
The New Guard: "Antivenom" (finalist for Knightville Poetry Contest)
Nimrod: "Question for the Dead," "Acrolect" (as "Rain on Leaf")
Notre Dame Review: "The Painters Who Were Not Masters"
Oxford Poetry: "Elegy for Several Selves"
Plough: "Wreath-Making" (finalist for Rhina P. Espaillat Poetry Award)
Poetry Wales: "Elephant in Hannibal's Army"
Slice: "Letter from a Roman Soldier in Gaul"
Subtropics: "The Storm Is What It Seems"
THEMA: "The Artist and His Collards"
Thrush: "Aubade"

I would like to thank the following teachers: Maggie Bailey, Dutton Kearney, William Logan, Ange Mlinko, and Michael Hofmann. Thank you Mark Jarman and Andrew Hudgins for encouragement at the right moment. Thank you Nick Pierce and Jake Grefenstette for your keen-eyed reading. Thank you, parents, for your grace and humanity. And thank you, Kayla Beth Moore, for sharing a life and a language with me.

Book design by Connie Amoroso

Library of Congress Control Number 2025938837
ISBN 978-0-88748-725-5

Printed and bound in the United States of America

10 9 8 7 6 5 4 3 2 1

for Kayla Beth and Penelope

Contents

iii.

"The mind, that ocean where each kind
Does straight its own resemblance find;
Yet it creates, transcending these,
Far other worlds, and other seas;
Annihilating all that's made
To a green thought in a green shade."

—Andrew Marvell, "The Garden"

Alpine Meadow

It only grows in high, elk-trampled fields
alongside flowers that take thirty years
to grow, and should it root, the soil is poor,
hail is frequent, and rain comes cutting cold.
The tourists yawn and drive into a cloud,
already bored by what eludes belief.
You have been looking for it all your life,
but are too ashamed to say its name aloud.
Goodness: archaic and embarrassing
as rhyme, fragile as an eyelid skin,
and just as loath to grow. Take a cutting
of the sorry thing, fly it home, coddle it in
a warm glass, and see: without ice
and wind and punishment, it dies.

Isaac's Memory

What I remember most is the desperate grin
my father wore, his lips retracted, his teeth
moon-white against the ruddy, fissured skin.
That smile said many strange things. Beneath
my father's horror, I saw a kind of joy
at finding God incoherent, the world absurd;
any god that asked a man to kill his boy
could not be reasoned with, dissolved all words,
and killed meaning, so Abraham was free
of me, and did not have to understand.
And when the bushes clattered with a ram,
a strange ambivalence warped his glee.
Before he took the gift, he freed my hands
and damned me to that glittering thought: "I am."

Wringing Lilies from the Acorn

To love a thing is to know a thing will die.
I know this, yet every March redbuds
shout, *Nothing dies!* Their vivid pseudo-lie
jams an acid hope between my ribs
as daffodils burst savagely through soil,
snapping yellow jaws. Titmice return.
We walk, shocked, into a plausible world
of things so ruthlessly alive they burn
our skin. We wonder, are we being mocked?
Is this a joke, this sudden burst of green?
No question's older or better. Books are packed
with autumn answers, crispy, rotten things,
and spring keeps roaring back, giving us
the test of joy, the one we'll never pass.

A Carcass

after Baudelaire

For many days it plagued our morning walk:
a German shepherd rotting in ragweed.
We watched it balloon with gas, a rounded shock
of fur, a hot and swollen bulb of feed

for buzzing, tiny fauna, and I do not think
we mentioned it aloud, just held our breath
to muzzle horror. Its luxuriant stink
elapsed; the skin collapsed; the bone beneath

blinked its dazzling fretwork at the sky.
We stared, tight-lipped. What were we to say?
Impossible to milk a moral from

that corpse. The fiercest facts preclude a Why.
Our helpless silence seemed the only way
to pray. The bones were eaten. Every crumb.

After Abel

I settled into the trees to wait for God.
Bullfrogs called, *Grow. Grow.*
Night's blue-black mist involved the air.

Oaks rimming the pond
basketed each twitch of shame.
When I opened my mouth to call out to God,
my throat opened to a bitter feast of stars.

Minnows, wrinkling the shallows,
worked over my reflected face
like the lips of Adonai.

I said, "If you can kiss me,
you can tell me where to go,"
but God said nothing.

Then a terrible fish, a phalanx of fins,
frolicked through the minnows.

I wish the killing had made me feel desolate,
but instead I exulted, smearing mud on my shoulders,
slapping the water for joy.

I slept on the shore,
and when I woke, I set out
in search of the land called Wandering.

Root Words

They say that trees can feel it when you walk.
Their fungal nerves are shuddering as your foot
thumps earth. They ponder you. A threat? They talk
about you, sending sugar through their roots,
uttering sugar-language, a grammar thick
as honey, in which every word is a root word,
and takes a week to say. A sentence trickles
over months. Conversations ooze in slurred
centuries. Long after you are dead,
they're still debating you. They recall
the pattern of your feet, the seedlings snapped
by your passage, what little difference you made.
Your name goes dark in human circles first.
It's held by trees a while. And then dispersed.

Antivenom

We should go back,
said the voice behind
your veil (an orange towel
wrapped around your head),

but I had seen a waterfall
on the valley's far rim,
and fresh curiosities
worked through my legs.

You straggled after me,
trampling the dry ruins
of old mesquite groves,
reciting under your voice

the names of rattlesnakes.
An arid sense of loss
trailed you, spicing the air
like the memory of smoke.

You even stumbled, somewhat
like an overripe Fantine
mourning the loss of her hair
through the deserts of Paris.

I pointed to a hiker deep
in the tawny void behind us.
Look at the size of his pack—
A ranger. They carry antivenom.

I had no idea if this was true,
and you remained unhappy.
Only the waterfall kept me
in the steady shade of hope.

I anticipated smooth rocks,
flattened by the river.
Finally the train of your grief
would gather at your ankles,

and I would kiss your wrist
and apologize for taking us
this far from air conditioning.
I'm writing all this because

today is your birthday,
and I can hardly recall
half of what I ought to.
Well, at least I can say

we never found the waterfall.
After the first arroyo,
the desert deepened,
and there was no noise

except for the rustle
sand makes when it's bored
and the dull whispering
of your rattlesnakes.

I knew I was culpable
and savored my culpability
like a gloom of water
splashed over bright sand.

Since then I've learned
when a pit viper gets you,
your blood thickens to black jelly
in the space of minutes.

A coagulant in the venom,
stored in the plump sacs
above their yellow eyes,
does the trick. These bites

are cleaner than most wounds.
If you cut a victim open, say
a foot or the back of a knee,
you'll find it makes no mess.

Only the worst bites require
antivenom, which works
by cluttering your molecules
and making you very sick,

I forget the details.
We were nearly married,
and I cannot remember
half of what I meant to.

Today I return to the hike
through cracked mesquite
to the dust-ghosted car,
listening to you work out

your grammar of desertion,
your spell for the season of fear:
Speckled, Tiger, Sidewinder,
Mojave, Pygmy, Diamondback.

In a Green Shade

Of all the things I fail to cultivate—
my will, my days—my barren, sandy yard
unearths me most. Its acid soil is hard
for temperate plants to bear; they curl and wait
for tropical death. Each day I wake and find
new wiltings: dry squash, exhausted thyme,
and, hidden by a leaf, coated with slime,
an aphid-plundered pepper, reduced to rind.
Yet weeds explode on skinny, taunting stalks,
or long stems that bend with lavish blooms,
to prove that nature thrums to certain words
which I will never speak. When green things talk,
I'm a child, ear pressed against his parents' room,
who hears some awful thing, but hears it blurred.

Elephant in Hannibal's Army

The trees are poison here. The stones bite,
cracking whitely under me, and slide
wetness into the fissures of my pads.
Uphill. Gray-white. Men make fires, lie down
in snow. Most rise. Not all. The mountain drowns
me in softness; the moldy Spanish straw they feed
me wriggles with rats; the heavenly air derides
my lowland lungs. The men pray for a fight.
Next dawn, we pass a smaller me, dawn-stiff,
bestrewn with butchering men who stuff bits
of trunk in saddlebags, cracking jokes. Far off,
the mountain shouts, and something frozen splits
inside me. My mind falls down, skies descend,
and all the uphill, hell-white world caves in.

Eating in a State of Flowers

In Florida, the pigs eat escargot,
the sluggish horses nibble Spanish moss,
the manatees hold feasts of watercress,
and I can manage only dry Bordeaux
before the steamed ricotta, basil, dough,
and garlic from my favorite pizza place.
I eat and watch the alligators pass
along the docks and sloops and gauche chateaux
of memory, their teeth as cold as stars.
One grips a buck and twists the antlered head.
Another chokes an egret in the mud.
Their young will watch our cities die
and calmly bob on time's erasing flood,
ignorant of America, outliving God.

Waiting for Birth

The world is sign-swollen. A luna moth
drops out of the sky, wet-winged, to dry
at your feet. Your belly bubbles: skull and knees.
All rounded things—the globes of trees,
strangers' eyes, a soapy lump of froth
in the sink—begin to thump expectantly,
as though a knot of chary mischief was balled
in every spheroid thing. Our child's breath
has never been. She's never used her voice.
Hope is absurd. An argument with death
is never won in rational terms. So we told
ourselves to plunge into the strangest choice
a man can make, struck a truce with loss,
went spinning into love's bizarre abyss.

Penelope, Growing Old

Paling at its peak, a wave crumples
to greening rush, dotted by the leaps

of panicked mullet. Fishermen shout;
winds carry the roar to the palace.

Feeding my husband a forkful of fish
I watch for ripples on his mien.

By now, he's lost the mind that made
him him. I cup his chin and work it

in slow circles. Odysseus can't chew.
My love pisses desultorily and often.

He recalls me less and less.
Some days he thinks I am his daughter

while I nurse him like my son. Today
he sleeps by the fire, deep in furs,

as termites graze our olive bed.
Each day I ask the end to hurry.

Meanwhile memory treads the hem
of my dress, saying, Look back, back

when jaws were firm, death a laugh,
and Odysseus was far away in Troy,

with Circe, becoming a pang,
a raging absence, and finally an idea,

a warm idea he killed by coming back.

Flaubert, Senility

"Remind me how it ends," she says.
I lower my book and watch her pupils
like creepers protruding past blindness,
rotating in the branchless dark.

They're uprooting from self, those eyes,
dimmed and arrested by whatever it is
that approaches.

Auto Nativity

Hunched and rummaging, they rearrange
their furtive cave of private air,
grasping deep for something I can't see.

Their heads are nestled in the dark.
Crumpled napkins snow to their feet.

It almost doesn't matter what they bring
out of the gloom—a purse, a gun, a comb—

It's the face they wear, the instant they lurch
back to the world, amazed by everything.
The way a child looks, fresh from the womb.

Not Knowing How to Breathe

Your breath against my ear, ten-pound girl,
is a blend of sighs and snorts, of jagged whirrs
and gurgle-moans. Teach me how to hear
you learning how to breathe. To mark the purl
of puff that gladdens orchards in the lungs.
The rattle-breath of hunger. The hiccup-sigh
of fullness. Not knowing how to breathe is a song;
soon you'll know, and this balky song will die.
You'll come to breathe in fluent, thoughtless gulps.
Voluble without attention, you'll take
refreshment without thanks. As I do. Help
me, ten-pound girl, hear your labored breath
for what it is. The slog of getting the gift.
The awkward, slow rowing away from death.

Wreath-Making

The hard, dark berries, blue as black
snakes are blue, befogged with newness, clench
their pips in scaly tufts of green, each branch
an elenchus of logic, a spray of craze, an attack

on soft fingers walking through them, your
fingers, calling shape from the bedlam of life
with brutal twists of form. You flick the knife
to smooth a stem, a cedar stem: its fur

heaps greenly on your shoes, as if you'd skinned
a woolly tree, not trimmed it, to make a wreath.
Finished circle made of endings, shaped

to hint what never ends, it tricks and bends
the eye to green forevers, clever deaths
of death, where girls and berries do escape.

Threnody

A girl screamed. The high, mechanical note
surged into my room with April sun
and catbird calls. Heartbeats hammered my throat;
I couldn't see her, so imaginary horrors ran
harrows through me: pistol, fist, torn skirt.
My fear was not for her. It was for me.
I did not want to witness blood and dirt
and desecration. When I went to see,
I found a man feeding chunks of wood
to a chop saw. The yellow pine wailed
as teeth unknit its grain. Embarrassment
burned my ears. For a long time I stood
in dapples. An odd ache said she was there.
Somehow inside the sound. Somehow aware.

Turning One

The moth-eyed girl is baffled, turning one,
by gangs of grins, by sudden song and cake.
Her face grows cloudy. An uncle's knuckles crack,
and she cries. Grins descend; soon she's done,
off to bed, where she lies in thickening gloom,
her mind a snarl of images: rustle-clumps
of wrapping paper, smoky candles, big thumps
of strange shoes. She's safe inside her room,
but what has happened to her? She does not know
the way of birthdays. She frets, dozes, dreams
of flocks of grins that caw and dive like crows.
One day she'll know too much. A self will grow
behind those eyes. One day all smiles will dim.
For now she sleeps. Her breaths are solemn-slow.

Killing Orpheus

After archers shoot Diana's dogs,
the slaves haul Actaeon's remains away
in wooden wheelbarrows. The crowd boos

as a criminal dressed as Orpheus appears
and trots to the center of the Coliseum,
weaving through wheelbarrows trickling red.

A balding Charon offers him a lyre.
The crowd, impatient and simmering, heckles hotly.
Children throw marbles of rolled-up bread.

Wheelbarrows disappear into the tunnel
as girls dressed like maenads begin to emerge.
One wears a leopard pelt. Her nose is running.

One wields a slender branch. One grips a sickle.
The one with the sickle looks ready. The one
with the branch can't keep her eyes open,

and her ivy crown keeps slipping down
over her eyes. Someone yells, "Play
a song!" and Orpheus scrambles to obey.

He motions for quiet with a fluttering hand.
He hunts a tune. His fingers stagger after it.
The crowd hushes. Patricians bend their ears,

but his voice is small, his shoulders flabby,
and that's what does him in. The boos begin.
Children stop throwing their marbles of bread

to watch him parry the sickle with his lyre.
They hear the squeal of cut strings, cheer
to see him helmeting his head with wine-

fat arms, to watch him drop in a storm of limbs.
Some complain the fight is rigged, unfair.
But when the sickle-girl moves in, they hush.

Each cut she makes is a marvel of efficiency.
Soon she swings Orpheus's head by a lock
of wet hair. The applause is loud and brief.

ii.

⁂

Aubade

All human lovers are far away.
Caught in the magnolia's cold arms,

the air is so still it makes the sap whine.
Night reveals the busy moods of love:

ants haul crumbs of lichen
on their humming black current.

Ankles brush through leaves
as dawn gets dressed in aching reds,

studying the mirror, whistling
like a murderess who's done this before.

Adam's Task

Before he named the world, Adam heard
the whorled languages of ferns, the hiss
and pop of wood, the quips of birds, the pure
elucidation of rivers combing moss.
And he would sit and listen, jealous, thick
with muted love. One day, with no warning,
a cork unstopped his throat. Greedy, quick,
the names flowed out. He shouted, floundering
through green, freshening the world with terms.
It lasted days. When it was done, his tongue
was cracked. He crawled to drink, noting how firm
the *earth,* the *bank*. He owned it now. The songs
of birds were passionless. Cold quiet soaked
the woods. He begged the trees. Now nothing spoke.

Acrolect

Listen to the dark vocabulary of rain.
Wind whips a shower from leaf-clouds:
the noise shatters sheets of glassy air,

and language forms
from water's cadence, lilting down to dirt,
a fracas of alien tongues.

If it's harm to speak a thing,
you cannot hurt this dialect.

The world is full of secrets of this kind:
languages too quick to eavesdrop,
glinting treasures that repel the mind.

Coffee Grounds

When the boy begins to pee incessantly—
leaving class, leaving dugouts, leaving bed—
black mold flourishes in the toilet. He grows
weak and thin, familiar with the exact
location of every water fountain at his school.

One morning his mother comes to wake him up.
He's pale as bedsheets, his eyes brown dots.
He can't relax his legs; the calves have seized.
She drives him to the hospital, and on the way
he vomits a coarse black substance webbed

with blood. *Coffee grounds* in medical parlance.
He is diagnosed with a common disease
and hooked to clear tubes pumping salt.
A handsome doctor says, You are too sweet.
Your blood and pee. Your sweetness is a poison.

The boy nods. This coheres. His sweetness
introduces him to families of pain—
headache uncles, panic aunts—and he
is relieved to meet them, learn them, say their names
out loud. Impatient with the general grief,

he leaves the room whenever someone cries.
In any other age he would be dead.
He roams new halls, marooned in foreign skin.
He slides bright needles into his arm and thigh.
He drifts into the tedium of miracles.

Startled by the Breaking Cup of Spring

The sun arranges branches, scattering crumbs
of light across the bed they used to share,
and it staggers grief, it churns the mud of prayer
to wonder where he is. His arm lay there.
He dozed with dust and brightness pouring
through that pane of pollen-crusted glass.
She makes the bed to smooth unruly time.
She straightens books and disinfects the desk.
She tidies things until they don't belong.

Dragonflies Hunting

Delicate acts make durable news.
This dragonfly that bends the stem
digests its prey to steep its blues.
Delicate acts make durable news:
as I wonder what I've said to you,
my throat becomes a subtle drum.
Delicate acts make durable news
and leave behind a shuddering stem.

Wild Azaleas

Last year, balanced on the brush of spring,
I found a craggy, pinkish bud whose name
I'd never learned. Its fleshy spikes became
a riddle, soft and strange, a nameless thing
that I took home and painted. Done, I hung
the painting on my wall so every day
I'd pass and pause and pluck that shivering string:
Here's something you don't know, which thrilled the way

a feeling thrills *because* you do not know
its name. A year went by. This afternoon
the bush was loud with frantic, orange-frilled
detonations. *Wild azaleas.* They glowed
with naming, becoming song, and to their tune
I buried something sweet that naming killed.

On the Nature of Yes

To what bright thing cocooned in me
does this yes correspond? I feel it quake
with life, growing large, growing wings.

A moth, a fly, a nymph. A slime of hope.
Pupa of happiness. Love's lashing grub.

The Rival

I lifted the wilted, heavy head of the sun-
flower to hunt its ruined face for seeds.
Snapping off a chunk, I pried my thumb
between the nestled shells, and in my greed
I didn't see a scampering beetle until
I'd severed his leg. In the brittle shade
of blackened petals, he waited for his world
to end. I filled my cheek with tender seeds
and watched him hide, wondering if he'd die.
Would he mourn the leg? And did it hurt?
Hornets clacked the grass like arid rain.
The beetle shrank and twitched, its tiny eyes
opaque, and gradually I felt the bite
of watching something feeling maybe pain.

Ophelia

after John Everett Millais

Incapable of our own distress, we cache
our doubt in her sodden marvel of a gown.
No death should ever be this beautiful.
Complicit in forget-me-nots, we drown
in the language of flowers, glory in the flash
of her cheek against dark wet. Her pallor pulls us

down to savage depths of white. Alive,
she'd be less wonderful. The model took
a four-month bath, fully clothed, and shook
with chills Millais ignored. Beauty thrives

in fevered minds. Ophelia infects
the facts we were so certain of; our heads
grow petal-rotten, and life seems incorrect.
We want our lush ghost. We want her dead.

Ringneck

We thought it was a worm: it bucked and thrashed
like one, scribbling black across the trail,
but then the tiny glint of polished scales
glissandoed up my spine. I almost crushed
its head, held back, and teased it with a stick.
It did not bite. It only crazed a course
through moss, vanishing and coming back
from darkness, its slender golden ring a curse
on stealth. A concession made to beauty, you mused:
a witty gem encrusting nature's grave
calculus of sex and death. Then again,
I didn't know. Perhaps the ring had a use.
I almost wondered if beauty was nature's slave—
a flash of coal-fire belly, and the snake was gone.

The Monster Captures Frankenstein

Unless a man refines his ear,
reason will slosh like *mal de mer;*
unless he's born with natural wit,

balancing on decks of rhetoric
will leave him queasy, scared to sail.
You are a small and queasy man

but you are also my father. This fact
yokes and goads my will. Get warm.
I will explain it all again.

The moment you made me
you became my slave. I hold you
as the ocean holds a fish.

I will not ask why you did it.
That would only plunge our heads
into a fog of rage and cause.

Instead I'll ask you why you fail
to comprehend a simple truth:
if you entwine a net of flesh

with warmth and sensibility,
you are caught in it for good.
Sit up, my Setebos, and reflect:

The hour you saw my yellow eyes
crack and complicate the dark
you were fettered in my net.

From rags of meat you stitched this I.
You coiled me around your arm;
you plucked these eyes from rotten heads.

You made me terrible to see.
While you, my architect, are soft
and handsome, a boy all bloom.

Don't shiver. I will throw a stump
on the fire. Let me look at you.
Your lips are a glow of tissue, yes,

each fingertip a soft pink belly.
Against the shambles you have raised
you're made of honeycomb and birch.

But I would not trade bodies with you.
I do not want to wear your clothes.
My hands, though pustulent and gray,

can tear through ice. My numb lips
crunch snow without a hint of sting.
You know what I can do to men.

Still shivering. Why? The fire's tall.
I've made you warm and safe but all
you do is sulk and shake and fail

to meet my eyes. Please, be a man.
Good. Now hold my gaze. I am
your greatest ambition satisfied.

It is no wonder you despise me.
I promised not to ask you why
you made me. Now I renege.

You flinch at every log that pops
and join each whimper of the wind.
Pull yourself together and explain:

You made a creature capable of hurt,
a creature capable, in other words,
of loving you, then crept away.

Why? Go on. I'll let you finish.
Mother, Father, Maker, God:
Untie your tongue. Amaze me. Speak.

iii.

* * *

Question for the Dead

Today I saw a squirrel with two ropes
of ants flowing rapidly out of its eyes.
Jasmine petals fell around the corpse.

Tell me how to live. Worm into my ear.
I want one instant of my life to be clear.

Reading Catullus in Bed

You snore against my arm, a zoo of dreams
that you'll forget tomorrow, one by one,
your skull's hinge creaking open. Alone
on the weird moon of consciousness, I warm
my eyes over the fire of Catullus,
his *pēdīcābo* coals, his withering ash,
smiling as I underline the louche,
smoking verse, savoring what is foolish
and wise in him. Your breath subdues my arm.
A cool rain taps the roof. A buttercup
unyellows on our sill. A siren howls.
Death seems weak tonight, remote as Rome,
held back by careful rhymes, by teeming sleep,
by the underlining pencil's quiet snarl.

Clew

The wind unfastened twigs from cedars; fleet
indigo berries bounced to where we read
together, dark globes leaping past our feet,

and then a clutch of drops, cold and sweet,
rolled down my neck, twitching out a thread
of thought. I grabbed it, felt it give a neat

sharp tug, hunger-dark and indiscreet,
and knew this moment's squall was almost dead,
but while it lasted I might hear the beat

of some more generous measure in the sheets
of rain, if I was quiet and listened hard—
I tried, I tried, until ears were obsolete,

but all I heard was snapping twigs and rain
then tumbled bankrupt into time again.

Sweetgum Ball

Spike-laden fruit, ant mansion, prickle-globe
of hollow darks, an orb despised by those
who treasure lawns, caltrops for human toes,
considered spiny litter, ignoble nub
of nature's unprofitable side, the sweetgum ball
is loved by kids with nothing else to throw.
I used to hoard them, hurl them at a wall
of white brick, rapt in the golden glow
of a task completely useless. They'd bunch
at the base, where concrete swallowed brick,
then decompose until the jolts of March,
when a hundred sweetgums sprouted fast and thick,
cracking bricks with young and swarming roots,
bright green choking out the white of use.

Stanzas for Dwoskin

Dwoskin taught me how to fold a box
around limber stalks of aluminum
and slash the cardboard with a penknife.
Then he shut his mind to me for the summer.

The floor became a sea of tedium,
schooled with sawdust and silver parings.
Foremen sailed by, sweat-slick and shouting
orders drowned by industrial fans.

As I got to know the diverse complaints
of worked metal, its muffled shrieks,
Dwoskin muttered to himself and thumbed
something secret in his shirt's dark pocket.

After lunch he'd come back out of breath,
forehead glittering with liquid thoughts.
If he leaned over me to reach his helmet,
I could smell him, and I was too young

to govern fear. Ten years is still too close.
I cannot measure what he was or meant
or meant to say on that thick afternoon
when he lifted the visor of his sullenness

and noticed the other rackers and packers
leaning into a phone's glow. One offered,
"That bitch in shape. She fuck wild."
The tone was soft, almost reverent.

Dwoskin stood up, about to speak,
and perhaps would have if a foreman
hadn't sailed along, belching orders.
Before too long, Dwoskin was done, fired.

I never knew why. He loathed me
and found conversation distasteful.
He was a factory of terrible thoughts.
I was the bossman's flaccid son.

What did kindness have to do with us?

The Painters Who Were Not Masters

Église Sainte-Croix, Bordeaux

I did not come to see the city's best.
Not for me the glitz of Saint-Seurin,
the pert discernment of le Grand-Théâtre.
Give me the crummy church, the jerry-built,
that dumpily broods in bright Bordeaux.

Who shot this gummy stump of Romanesque
into the sky of Aquitaine? Abadie did that.
Monsieur Abadie, architect of imbalance,
restored medieval churches in Bordeaux
with scant regard for taste or accuracy,

so now Église Sainte-Croix stands half-and-half:
half Gothic grunt, half Second Empire sigh,
a Frankenstein's Eglise, a funky mutt,
and after four espressos I cross the square
to see what paintings decorate the church.

I do the bovine dance of those in France
who visit churches: once around the aisles,
hands concatenated on the rump,
easing a hoof or two into the chapels
—in search of what?

Some holy flash? Half an hour killed?
I do not know, but what I find is sheer
shabbiness. And this is what enthralls
my heart. The unconvincing paintings, yawns
in oil, go vague and crackly with neglect.

There is a bleeding Christ who does not suffer,
a lacrimating Mary who does not grieve.
Deformed angels leer uselessly from a cloud.
The paintings touch me with their clumsiness,
moving me because they fail to move.

Every age must have its unmasterly masters,
those who simply lack the gift. They are
the vast majority of us who write
or paint, who faintly feel the jabbing fact:
I am the gesso on the board, the glue;

the habitat of genius, not its warm
and darting spark. Feeding years to hope,
loving well what does not love them back,
they labor and strop. It makes no difference.
Their ardors never get it right. Their news

is never news, their truth a jaundiced lie.
Out of pity (telling myself it's pity,
afraid I understand) I try to memorize
their names, these almost men, these yesterdays.
But as I leave, I'm dazzled by the day,

and almost trample a waiter. He collects
his legs, espressos jiggling on his tray,
mutters, *"Presque!"* and is right. How close
they were, those men. How hot on beauty's heels.
The almost men. The flightless, staring angels.

The Storm Is What It Seems

"Let be be finale of seem."
—Wallace Stevens

Chunks of atmosphere tear
wetly past. Oaks scream taut.
Owls hunker down in rot
holes. The rain's a net

too slight to slow the bucking trees,
unraveling by slow
degrees, that catches only gleams
of leaves. All we know

of rain is dry. What's dryly true
is false when rain's wet reign
begins to pluck the puckering dust.
Our knowing is a stain

no rain can rinse. The rancid brain
fogs up with knowing steam,
a mold of words infects the skull
and makes the storm a seam

through which a commentary pours,
a second flood of dreams
that drowns the birds inside their trees,
swamping is with seems,

until a bluebird magics past,
whose name is blue, whose wings
unfold, dissect, absolve, who seems
and seems until he sings.

Ambivalence of Birds

The beak, the claw, the green reptilian eye
induce the wind to mindless buoyancy,
and we, whose bodies crave the clutch and clog
of soil, sew our thoughts into their wings.
We'd love to slice the air, to slip our slog
and scythe through fog, but birds are fickle things:
they're fragile, too. One morning in my yard
a window thudded, so softly it seemed shy.
I saw a blur of blue descend, land hard
and lie, an iridescent flake of sky
spasming on the stair. It fanned its tail,
one final spray of nerves, and died in terror.
It hit the glass not knowing itself. It failed
to stop itself from rushing to the mirror.

The Artist and His Collards

"Jesse Aaron"
Photographer Unknown.
c.1970

The photographer must have posed him this way:
arms out behind a lavish plume of gray leaves,
he wraps his arms almost around abundance.
Alone in the gallery, I hypothesize collards,
or kale of tremendous size. Bug-chewed,
their holes make the leaves resemble living lace.

The sculptures, comfortably modern in their rage
to express, have gash mouths and depthless eyes.
Aaron's face is ambiguous—something withheld—
but his hands are the midwives of profusion.
In the guest book, a visitor writes primly in green ink,
"I try to never second-guess the curator."

The Albert Memorial

It takes a special zest to gore the clouds,
to slice the teeming world in marble fourths:
America, a bison primly bowed;
Europe, aurochs sillier than a corpse;
Africa, a camel trying to spit;
and Asia, that overheated elephant.

But you look uncertain, draped in gold,
caught in your airy cage of caryatids
and staring out at heaps of sullen wealth:
the marrow scraped and sucked from Egypt's spine.
Did you ever hear, tapping on your shelf,
the long white stick of unmalicious time?

Humdrumming

Sunlight cakes the earth like something thick,
like something you could sink your fingers in,
like something that could stain your cleanest shirt.
Turkey vultures hang, waiting for the nick
of time to plummet them. Flags snap at wind.
Children lift their vulgar shouts and flirt
with shade, chasing shrieks from pine to pine.
Peeling back the unremarkable,
I wet my hands in the plodding miracle
of light and shade, of single file lines,
of beer cans jangling down the empty street,
of all the prosy things that make a world,
and hear a humdrumming, a daily beat
that measures us, trembling through the void.

Come to Grief

Young for now, almost wholly well, my wife
takes bread out of the oven and taps the crust
to test its give. It crackles, coughing just
a little steam. Then back to oven life.
She walks outside to watch a yellow shelf
of clouds gleam through our silver, molting oak.
The sky does not return her cordial look.
Will grief come to me or I to grief?
Some hell is coming. Nothing I can do.
The bread is close. The night is now. I can't
be glad, and must. This crumb of time, this whiff
of almost-ready bread, is all that's true
and good for me, or all that I can stand.
She darts inside and pats the crisping loaf.

Biking the Dog

Churning his bike, the dog galloping beside,
(obedient shepherd, bracketed by wheels)
a man has hammered his chore into a blade
of grace that eviscerates the day and reveals

two gleams of locomotion—the blur of spin,
the sudden spring and snap of legs—two verbs
that whisk the morning into froth, and send
a quivering thrill across the drowsy universe

of habit. They're gone now. My coffee's cold.
The neighborhood goes back to sleep, but I
have seen a skillful thing, a jewel made

from nothing, and so, before the feeling's old,
I return to the page with sharpened eyes,
a little more serious, a little more afraid.

Gall

A dainty, speckled orb, a subtle fig,
pink as the pith of an idea, a plum
gall sheds shocking purple blood when cut.
You stain your palm wondering where it's from,
peering up into sieving green. Ripe nuts
crack beneath your boot. You take a twig

and pry: a larva, fish-belly-white and stiff,
tumbles from the core of violet flesh.
Its larval stillness, sheer and cold, is the stuff
of fear. It pursues you into sleep like a wish.

That night, you envision every fruit on earth
cracking open to release buzzing streams
of wasps. You must expect some awful birth
from every ripe, beguiling, gentle dream.

Minnows

Beside the slap and gurgle of a stream,
in one of those sequestered green
pools, unsanitary with light, swim
fish too small, too slender-bright, to mean
much more than sift and sand. Their bulbous eyes
and beating tails are clear as twisted glass,
and dimly gleam in sullen, mud-gold rays.
They wouldn't feed a fly, their mass less
than a line of floss, and yet they satisfy
some murky need in me to see a crumb
of light go struggling to an edge and ram
into a flowing dark. It's an anodyne
for nameless pains to watch them come to grief
against a drift that wouldn't move a leaf.

Smoke Jumper

1.

He stepped across the metal ramp and fell,
feeling his stomach vanish as he pierced
the first tower of smoke. Coughing at the smell
of heat-burst pines, he yanked the cord, first
to jump, and entered a cleaner tube of air.
He was not thinking of his wife back home.
He was not thinking of his plummeting crew.
He had no thoughts as he spiraled through
hot ash, watching each detail acutely bloom
below: serrated ridge of scrambled rocks,
bellies and bulbs of smoke, a copse that birthed
one quick, jabbing tongue of yellow flame.
Having no thoughts, he had joy. Until a shock
climbed his boots. Remarried to the earth,
he rose in a place where nothing knew his name.

2.

The burning valley belched a charcoal smear.
Divided from his crew by vines of smoke,
he was lost. His breath was ash; he soaked
his hair with bottled water. Stiff with fear,
he had the vibrant sense of being prey
to something igneous and implacable.
He thought he glimpsed a shape, obscured by scree,
and wrapped his fingers around his red shovel.
It was a cougar's corpse, burnt alive
and bramble caught. Thorns transfixed its pose:
snarling, tendons cooked, coiled to dive
at a mute monster of heat. The fire had frozen
its eyes; empty sockets blazed raw dark.
Something seemed to stir within that murk.

3.

Gloom where God or light or laughter lurked.
The man drew back, and raised his shovel to strike
the dark, to douse the eyes, but a spike
of wonder pierced his heart. His mind worked.
He sat on ashen rocks to consider the cat.
Its sharp carnivorous pose reminded the man
of nothing in particular, but it spat
ancient pictures deep into his brain:
Moses, rancid toothed and dying, banned
from Canaan, cursing feebly at his God.
And Cain, pale and sweat slick, flinging clods
of soil across a mound, using sand
to plug the vacant eyes, begging like a child:
Wake up, wake up. The images were cold

4.

and wild but he endured them, still unsure
if he was seeing anything real, or just
a fear collage, a spasm of his mind.
He had the urge again, hot as lust,
to smash the eyes, but underneath that rind
he sensed a kind of innocence, a bizarre
affection, rising for the dead and noble thing.
His vision blurred. Then sudden chuckles and cries
destroyed his solitude. Steps crunched higher.
His crew arrived, their voices flushed with fire.
They looped around him. He rubbed his eyes.
They asked where he'd been. Feeling the sting
of their camaraderie, he could not speak.
They offered sandwiches whose onions reeked.

5.

Chewing together, at ease, they asked again.
He hesitated, nodded at the corpse.
They squinted, cried out. One hauled the warped
body out of thorns. One scratched its chin
and laughed, flashing half-chewed bread.
The man felt a hot froth of anger rise
and seal his throat. He held the shovel head
and squeezed his hatred out. The cougar's eyes,
those darkly knowing pits, seemed to bid
him rise, attack. Commanded him to strike
his crew and scatter them. The moment bled
away. He did nothing. Then someone took
a Pulaski. Chopped into the charred neck.
The head detached, fell, bounced through rocks.

6.

When he got home, he tried to tell his wife
about the corpse, about the dark where God
had lurked and laughed, but some mute thief
stole the substance from his words, and cold
incomprehension hardened on her face.
Owlish and tall, she loathed the hint of smoke,
and hid her amber teeth whenever she spoke.
Hearing her husband's voice, she felt erased,
cheated of tenderness, because he'd failed
to ask about the days when he'd been gone.
She tried to chasten him with barbed looks.
She cannot hear, he fumed. Faces pale,
they fought, alone in a suddenly alien room,
and went apart to think identical thoughts.

7.

Storming out to pace beneath the pines,
she felt the needles under her feet bend
and crack, wondering what crude design
had fastened her to this particular man,
to this irascible place and feeble self.
Her loneliness was threadbare now. Not bright
and tragic as it used to be. If she sniffed
her ardors, they were odorless. A light
misting rain depressed the silent pines.
Her nape-stuck hair passed transparent beads
along its length. Soon he'd leave again.
Nothing mattered. There was in him a greed
she could not name. Hounding signs from God,
he pulled a Christ from every clump of mud.

8.

He could not see the wife, alive and real
before him, who did not ask for God or light,
but only craved an hour of words, a night
of true and chiming talk, to make her feel
like she existed, so air would have to part
around her form. Toes gouged the earth.
When each person dies, is there really a heart
that beats differently? She was alert.
Awake to rain. The sky tore down a shower.
In those descending globes she sensed a clue,
some uncanny answer dappling her solitude.
Before she netted it in words, the power
withdrew. Her shirt was soaked. She was cold.
She walked home, brewed tea, and grew old.

Letter from a Roman Soldier in Gaul

Dear X,

Assigned at last to join the army's ranks,
I pecked my mother's nose and sped to Gaul
where I found my century thundering drunk
and torturing a naked man, a tall
prisoner named Diorix. Cheering, they lashed
him to a horse and chased it off a scarp
to hear how wail and whinny splash
the ear as a single sound, flute-pure and sharp
as tarts from Carthage. "And now you can't
deny you've heard a Gallic centaur yell!"
Laughter. Rations. Kindling. Life at camp.
These men could be my friends; they treat me well.
We only argue what "Caesar" originally meant.
"Good hair." "Bright eyes." "Butcher of elephants."

Elegy for Several Selves

I am the place that person used to live.
I am the drowning victim's final lurch.
I am the broth that bubbles through a sieve,
the hue of children's voices in a church.
But then I'm pothos sprouting from a glass
and stapled to the wall, a boneless Christ.
Or maybe seedpods beaten from your dress,
or the muddy face a mother washes twice
and warms against her neck. I am a word
that used to mean, "raspberries plucked in mist"
but now denotes, "the fossil of a bird
found pressed in plates of cold Cretaceous schist."
And you, my love, are nothing on this earth
if not the crushing blank that ends my work.

Notes

"Startled by the Breaking Cup of Spring:" The title is lifted from a Song Dynasty poem by Li Ch'ing-Chao (Anglicized today as Li Qingzhao), translated by Kenneth Rexroth and Ling Chung.

"Smoke Jumper:" Smoke jumpers are wildland firefighters who leap from planes and drift down on parachutes to fight remote wildfires.

"Wringing Lilies from the Acorn:" The poem's title is lifted from Ezra Pound's "Hugh Selwyn Mauberley."

Previous titles in the Carnegie Mellon Poetry Series

2013
Oregon, Henry Carlile
Selvage, Donna Johnson
At the Autopsy of Vaslav Nijinksy, Bridget Lowe
Silvertone, Dzvinia Orlowsky
Fibonacci Batman: New & Selected Poems (1991–2011), Maureen Seaton
When We Were Cherished, Eve Shelnutt
The Fortunate Era, Arthur Smith
Birds of the Air, David Yezzi

2014
Night Bus to the Afterlife, Peter Cooley
Alexandria, Jasmine Bailey
Dear Gravity, Gregory Djanikian
Pretenders, Jeff Friedman
How I Went Red, Maggie Glover
All That Might Be Done, Samuel Green
Man, Ricardo Pau-Llosa
The Wingless, Cecilia Llompart

2015
The Octopus Game, Nicky Beer
The Voices, Michael Dennis Browne
Domestic Garden, John Hoppenthaler
We Mammals in Hospitable Times, Jynne Dilling Martin
And His Orchestra, Benjamin Paloff
Know Thyself, Joyce Peseroff
cadabra, Dan Rosenberg
The Long Haul, Vern Rutsala
Bartram's Garden, Eleanor Stanford

2016

Something Sinister, Hayan Charara
The Spokes of Venus, Rebecca Morgan Frank
Adult Swim, Heather Hartley
Swastika into Lotus, Richard Katrovas
The Nomenclature of Small Things, Lynn Pedersen
Hundred-Year Wave, Rachel Richardson
Where Are We in This Story, Sarah Rosenblatt
Inside Job, John Skoyles
Suddenly It's Evening: Selected Poems, John Skoyles

2017

Disappeared, Jasmine V. Bailey
Custody of the Eyes, Kimberly Burwick
Dream of the Gone-From City, Barbara Edelman
Sometimes We're All Living in a Foreign Country, Rebecca Morgan Frank
Rowing with Wings, James Harms
Windthrow, K. A. Hays
We Were Once Here, Michael McFee
Kingdom, Joseph Millar
The Histories, Jason Whitmarsh

2018

World Without Finishing, Peter Cooley
May Is an Island, Jonathan Johnson
The End of Spectacle, Virginia Konchan
Big Windows, Lauren Moseley
Bad Harvest, Dzvinia Orlowsky
The Turning, Ricardo Pau-Llosa
Immortal Village, Kathryn Rhett
No Beautiful, Anne Marie Rooney
Last City, Brian Sneeden
Imaginal Marriage, Eleanor Stanford
Black Sea, David Yezzi

2019

The Complaints, W. S. Di Piero
Brightword, Kimberly Burwick
Ordinary Chaos, Kimberly Kruge
Blue Flame, Emily Pettit
Afterswarm, Margot Schilpp

2020

Build Me a Boat: Words for Music 1968–2018, Michael Dennis Browne
Sojourners of the In-Between, Gregory Djanikian
The Marksman, Jeff Friedman
Disturbing the Light, Samuel Green
Any God Will Do, Virginia Konchan
My Second Work, Bridget Lowe
Flourish, Dora Malech
Petition, Joyce Peseroff
Take Nothing, Deborah Pope

2021

The One Certain Thing, Peter Cooley
The Knives We Need, Nava EtShalom
Oh You Robot Saints!, Rebecca Morgan Frank
Dark Harvest: New & Selected Poems, 2001–2020, Joseph Millar
Glorious Veils of Diane, Rainie Oet
Yes and No, John Skoyles

2022

Out Beyond the Land, Kimberly Burwick
All the Hanging Wrenches, Barbara Edelman
Anthropocene Lullaby, K. A. Hays
The Woman with a Cat on Her Shoulder, Richard Katrovas
Bel Canto, Virginia Konchan
There's Something They're Not Telling Us, Kimberly Kruge
A Long Time to Be Gone, Michael McFee
Bassinet, Dan Rosenberg

2023

Night Wing over Metropolitan Area, John Hoppenthaler
Phone Ringing in a Dark House, Rolly Kent
Fleeing Actium, Ricardo Pau-Llosa
Approximate Body, Danielle Pieratti
Wild Liar, Deborah Pope
Joy Ride, Ron Slate
That Other Life, Joyce Sutphen
Sonnets with Two Torches and One Cliff, Robert Thomas

2024

Accounting for the Dark, Peter Cooley
Shine, Joseph Millar
Those Absences Now Closest, Dzvinia Orlowsky
Blue Yodel, Eleanor Stanford
Her Breath on the Window, Karenmaria Subach
Museum of the Soon to Depart, Andy Young

2025

Just About Anything: New and Selected Poems, Jonathan Aaron
The End of the Clockwork Universe, Fleda Brown
Goat-Footed Gods, Kathleen Driskell
Pine, Jonathan Johnson
Requiem, Virginia Konchan
Angel Sharpening Its Beak, Michael McGriff
Trying x Trying, Dora Malech
Markers and Shrines, Margot Schilpp